I0146317

Milton Whitney

A Preliminary Report on the Soils of Florida

Milton Whitney

A Preliminary Report on the Soils of Florida

ISBN/EAN: 9783744759519

Printed in Europe, USA, Canada, Australia, Japan

Cover: Foto ©ninafisch / pixelio.de

More available books at **www.hansebooks.com**

BULLETIN No. 13.   S. 15.

U. S. DEPARTMENT OF AGRICULTURE.

DIVISION OF SOILS.

A PRELIMINARY REPORT

ON

THE SOILS OF FLORIDA.

BY

MILTON WHITNEY,

Chief of Division of Soils.

WASHINGTON:

GOVERNMENT PRINTING OFFICE,

1898.

LETTER OF TRANSMITTAL.

U. S. DEPARTMENT OF AGRICULTURE,
DIVISION OF SOILS,
Washington, D. C., February 26, 1898.

SIR: I have the honor to transmit herewith a preliminary report upon investigations of the principal soil formations of Florida, and to recommend that it be published as Bulletin No. 13 of this Division.

Respectfully.

MILTON WHITNEY,
Chief of Division.

Hon. JAMES WILSON,
Secretary of Agriculture.

2

CONTENTS.

	Page.
Introduction	7
Description of the soils and vegetation of the different formations	8
Pine lands	8
Truck growing	9
Hammock lands	11
Tobacco growing on the peninsula of Florida	12
Etonia scrub lands	14
Pineapple land	16
Lafayette formation of western Florida	17
Comparison of the different types of Florida soils	18
Texture of the soils	18
Chemical composition of the soils	20
Soluble salt content of soils	21
Moisture content of Florida soils	22

3

ILLUSTRATIONS.

PLATES.

Page.

PLATE   I. Characteristic growth of first quality of high pine land at Fort
     Meade 8
   II. Characteristic growth of second quality of high pine land at
     Altoona.. 10
  III. Characteristic growth of hammock land at Fort Meade 12
  IV. Method of irrigating tobacco land at Fort Meade 14
   V. Showing the contact of the scrub with the high pine land at
     Altoona.. 14
  VI. Characteristic growth of Etonia scrub at Altoona................. 16

TEXT FIGURES.

FIG. 1. Diagram showing moisture content of the hammock soils at Fort
    Meade and high pine soil at Winterhaven 25
    2. Diagram showing influence of half shading in conserving moisture
    in pineapple land at West Palmbeach during the dry season......... 26
    3. Diagram showing influence of half shading during the rainy season... 26

5

A PRELIMINARY REPORT ON THE SOILS OF FLORIDA.

INTRODUCTION.

In January, 1897, a reconnoissance trip was taken over Florida in order to make a preliminary study of some of the important soils and soil conditions of the State.

The principal types of soils examined were the first, second, and third quality of high pine land; the pine flats or so-called "flat woods"; the light hammock, the gray or heavy hammock, the mixed land, the heavy marl hammock; the pineapple land; the Etonia scrub, the spruce-pine scrub; and the Lafayette formation.

The principal localities and interests examined were the truck areas around Gainesville, Ocala, Orlando, Grand Island, Bartow, and Fort Meade; the tobacco areas of the Lafayette or "red-land" formation at Quincy, as well as the new tobacco areas at Ocala, Bartow, and Fort Meade; the pineapple districts at Orlando, Winterhaven, and along the east coast from Fort Pierce to Palmbeach; also the extensive scrub lands at Altoona known as the Etonia scrub.

There is a very marked difference in the character of the native vegetation on the different types of soil in the State. The hammock land, considered the most valuable for general purposes, has a more or less heavy growth of white oak, live oak, water oak, bay, hickory, magnolia, and dogwood, so dense at times as to form a veritable jungle. The white oak is found only on the very best hammock lands, while the red oak and the long-leaf pine grow together on what is called the mixed lands. The high pine land and the pine flats, as the names imply, contain a monotonous growth of long-leaf or spruce pine, the character of the land having a great influence upon the forest growth.

There is, as a rule, a more or less marked difference in the appearance of the soils of these different types of land, but notwithstanding the very great difference in the character of the vegetation on the hammock and pine land soil no appreciable difference has yet been found either from a chemical analysis or from an examination of the physical texture of the soils.

A brief description of the principal types of soil and the characteristic vegetation will be given, then a discussion of the chemical composition, of the physical texture, and lastly the water content of these soils will be considered with reference to the marked difference in the agricultural value.

7

DESCRIPTION OF THE SOILS AND VEGETATION OF THE DIFFERENT FORMATIONS.

PINE LANDS.

There are four important grades of pine land in the State—the pine flats or flat woods, and the first, second, and third quality of high pine land.

The soils of the pine flats have not been particularly examined, as they need underdrainage in order to make them at all productive. Besides being an expensive operation, this is at times an exceedingly difficult one on account of the flatness of the country and the slight fall which can be obtained to carry off the surplus water. The growth on the pine flats consists of the long-leaf pine, palmetto and grasses. The woods are open and very irregular in density; the soils are generally wet, with standing water from 1 to 4 feet below the surface. But few attempts have been made to reclaim or cultivate these flat woods on any extensive scale.

The first quality of pine land occurs only in small areas. It has a dark, rich, light sandy soil, in which a stick can often be pushed with ease to a depth of 2 or 3 feet below the surface. It has a very dense growth of long-leaf pine, so dense in fact that the trees are small, and for this reason it is frequently called "sapling" land. Plate I shows the characteristic growth of this land.

The soil, though loose and open like a garden soil in excellent tilth, holds together well, and has the property of taking any impression when molded in the hand, as a good quality of molding sand does. On drying it is not inclined to fall apart to a loose, incoherent condition, and roads through it have generally a compact, hard surface, very easy for traveling. This soil is very similar to the hammock and is considered quite as valuable as the hammock land for general agricultural purposes. What is said later in relation to the moisture of hammock soil probably applies to this also.

The second quality of high pine land covers vast areas in the peninsula. It is a very light, rather coarse, sandy soil, less coherent than the hammock or first quality of pine land. Still the roads through it are good. The characteristic growth is the long-leaf pine. The trees are sparsely set and often of quite large size. There is very little undergrowth, and a wagon or carriage can be driven through the forest in almost any direction. There is generally a good growth of grass, and these lands are very extensively used for grazing. Plate II shows the characteristic growth of this land.

These second quality high pine lands form the principal truck areas at Gainesville, Orlando, Winterhaven, Grand Island, and Bartow. The country is generally rolling, with differences of elevation of from 25 to 50 feet. The whole elevation of the lake region, which is extensively used for truck growing, is from 100 to 200 feet above sea level. The

PLATE I.

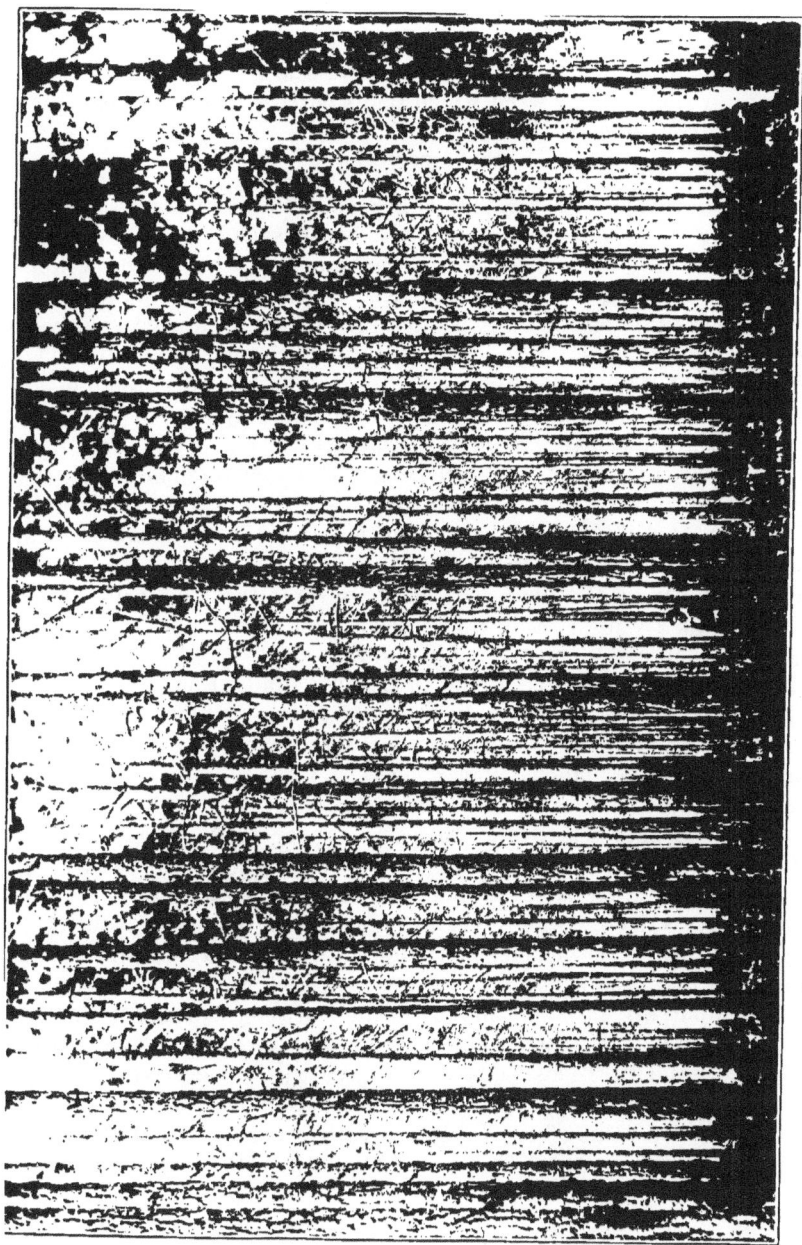

CHARACTERISTIC GROWTH OF FIRST QUALITY HIGH PINE LAND AT FORT MEADE.

soil is a coarse white or yellow sand, underlaid by a coarse, sandy sub-soil. It looks like a barren sea sand or a coarse, sharp, building sand, but that it is very productive is shown by the large and vigorous growth of pines, the luxuriant growth of grass, the great quantity of truck crops which can be produced during the season, and the enormous growth of beggar weed which takes possession of the land after the crops are removed.

TRUCK GROWING.

These second quality high pine land soils seem particularly adapted to truck growing. The climate of the region is such that the crops can be grown during the winter and placed upon the Northern markets during the winter and early spring. The winter months constitute the dry season of this locality. A particularly valuable property of these soils is the evenness of the water supply which they maintain. The surface of the ground quickly dries after a rain, and for a depth of an inch or two it is soon as dry as dust. Immediately below this depth, however, the sand is always moist. Truck crops seldom suffer on these soils from drought. It is claimed that in one year a crop of tomatoes was secured with but 1 inch of rain from the planting to the harvesting of the crop. Certainly a dry period which would cause a most disastrous drought upon the soils at the North appears to have hardly any effect on the crops of these truck soils. Several weeks after a rain the soil immediately under the dry surface is so moist that it will hold together when molded in the hand.

Four per cent of water seems to be an abundant supply for these truck lands, and 6 per cent makes the soil quite wet. During the past season the water supply in the soil at Winterhaven, at a depth of 3 to 6 inches, has never fallen below 3 per cent, although there have been periods of fifteen or twenty days without rain.

No reason can be assigned for the peculiar property these soils possess which enables them to maintain such a uniform water content. The soils are comparatively high, and the wells throughout the area are comparatively deep. Standing water is found on the average about 15 or 20 feet below the surface of the ground. Nowhere in the Eastern States are there soils similar to these where such a uniform water supply can apparently be maintained regardless of the frequency or amount of the rainfall. There are, however, in the Northwest, in southern California, and in Texas, soils which have this same power of withstanding drought to an even more marked extent than these high pine land soils. On some of these western soils it is no unusual thing for crops to thrive for a period of five or six months without rain and without irrigation.

Nearly every important variety of truck crops is grown upon these soils. The crops are planted usually from September to January, and are harvested and shipped north from November to the middle of April. The best market of the year is naturally from about the middle of March to the middle of April, and during this period the shipping of truck northward is at its height.

It has been pointed out in other publications that the production and marketing of truck crops is a matter of very great expense. It is only by intensive methods of cultivation, the forcing of a large yield from a small area, and the ripening and marketing of the crop during the winter and early spring months, when there is no competition from the Northern soils, that the industry can be made to pay the high freight charges for hauling the tender and bulky products the great distance they have to go.

The combination of climate and soil offer, in the main, ideal conditions for truck farming. Unfortunately, however, there is danger of an occasional frost which injures or destroys the first planting of the truck crop and, besides entailing loss with the necessity of replanting, makes the crop late, which is a far more serious consideration owing to the competition which it is likely to meet from the more northern localities. On account of this danger from frost the favored localities in the lake region and the extreme south of Florida, which are in a large measure protected by the influence of the water, have exceptional value for this truck industry.

The truck interests in the State as a whole are so large and the system of cultivation is so intense, there is so much of value on a comparatively small area, and the frosts come so rarely, that it certainly seems as if adequate measures of protection could be provided to insure the crop against loss. There are methods of smudges and ways of creating currents of air, and of heating the air itself, which would probably be very efficient and quite economical if applied on a large scale in the truck fields. Two or three times a year there is danger from frosts or freezes when, if the air could be moderately agitated, if a covering of smoke could be thrown up from a field, or if the air itself could be directly heated and raised about 5 or 8 degrees in temperature, the crops could be saved. Without this protection the risks are undoubtedly very great.

The principal crops are handled in about the following way: Tomatoes are planted from September to January, and the crop is shipped north from November till the middle of April. Eggplants have about the same season of growth. Eggplants are extremely difficult to start, but they, together with green peppers, are considered the most profitable crops that are grown. Peppers last from two to three years, when the plant needs to be renewed. Strawberries are grown upon the lower and more moist lands near the lakes, the season being from the middle of January to the middle of May. Beans are planted from September to January, and are shipped from November to April. Onions are shipped from September to January; cauliflower seems to be rarely grown; cabbage is also but little grown upon these high pine lands, but very extensively produced upon the heavy hammocks and the clay

PLATE II.

CHARACTERISTIC GROWTH OF SECOND QUALITY HIGH PINE LAND AT ALTOONA.

or marl hammocks. Peas are planted from September to March, and are shipped about six or eight weeks after planting. Sweet potatoes are planted from March to August, and mature throughout the year. Watermelons are planted from January to March, and are shipped from May to July. Irish potatoes are planted from September to the middle of January, and are shipped from the first of December to the middle of April. Celery is planted from September to January, and shipped from February to May.

As a rule, the truck soils are not occupied during the summer, and are allowed to grow up in crab-grass and beggar-weed, which produce an enormous growth beneficial to the soil and provide large cuttings of very nutritious hay. They are annual plants, and are well out of the way before the truck crops are put in. It is an advantage to have the soil thus protected during the summer time, and to have the organic matter added to the soil by the refuse is clearly an advantage to the plants.

The illustration, Plate II, is a characteristic view in second quality high pine land and, in contrast with Plate I, shows the marked difference in the character of the native vegetation on the first and second quality of land.

The third quality of high pine land consists of very loose and incoherent sand which on drying falls apart, so that the roads are exceedingly sandy and heavy for teams. The native growth of pine has little value. The soil is very poor and is not generally considered fit for cultivation.

HAMMOCK LANDS.

As already explained, the hammock lands are characterized by a native growth of hard-wood trees, principally of oak, hickory, magnolia, dogwood, and the cabbage palmetto. There are quite a number of grades of hammock land, distinguished by the kind and density of the growth, as well as by the character of the soil. There are light and heavy hammocks, so named from the density of the growth rather than from any appreciable difference in the character of the soil. The low, flat hammock, the high hammock, the heavy clay hammock, and the marl hammock, the various grades differing somewhat in the kind and relative proportion of the native trees.

As indicated by the name there is considerable difference in the texture of some of the hammock soils, but by far the largest area which has been studied consists of the light hammock and the heavy gray hammock, between which there is no apparent difference in texture. The soil and subsoil of these two hammocks consist of a moderately fine sand. The heavy hammocks are very dark colored, from the accumulation of organic matter from the dense growth which they have maintained in the past. This black soil is light and porous, and has the tilth of an excellent garden mold. It has a depth of from 1 to 3 feet.

These hammock lands are considered the most valuable in the State for general agricultural purposes. For special industries, however, especially for pineapples and some of the early truck crops, some of the other types of soil in the State have a higher value. The hammock soil at Fort Meade maintains about 8 per cent of water on the average, which is about twice as much as the high pine land truck soils at Winterhaven maintain. It seems strange, indeed, to a person familiar with the soils of the Northern and Western States, to see such a luxuriant growth of oak, hickory, and other hard wood trees on such light, sandy soil as this. The illustration, Plate III, gives some idea of the density of the growth on one of the heavy hammocks.

TOBACCO GROWING ON THE PENINSULA OF FLORIDA.

It was upon the heavy hammock land at Fort Meade that the tobacco industry received such an impetus about two years ago in the establishment of the Cuban colony at that place. Since then the industry has spread over all of the central portion of the peninsula, and has been developed upon all grades of hammock and pine lands.

The industry is so new that there is very little experience to draw from as yet in judging of what may be accomplished in the future. There is, however, much of promise in the results so far attained, and so much interest has lately been aroused in the subject of tobacco culture that a short statement of the conditions will not be out of the way.

It will be shown further along that, while this hammock soil maintains about twice as much moisture on the average as the second quality high pine land, the supply is not so uniform, and is subject to much greater variation, so that the crop is much more liable to drought. Tobacco is a plant which must be kept growing continuously. Any check is liable to change the character of the leaf, and for the cigar wrapper this is particularly undesirable. For the production of a fine, mild wrapper leaf it is necessary that the plant should receive no setback; for any check due to lack of moisture or of sufficient food material will tend to toughen the leaf, make it less elastic, and stronger when it is finally cured.

The filler leaf should be much stronger than the wrapper, as it forms the bulk of the cigar, and should determine the character. It is a mistake to suppose that equally good wrappers and fillers can be produced on the same plant. They should be treated differently from the very first. The filler should be raised upon a heavier, richer soil; and the plant produces a stronger, richer leaf if it is subjected to reasonable variations in the conditions of growth. The plants intended for filler leaves can be advantageously planted closer together, the soil can be manured much more heavily, the cultivation need not be so thorough, and a much heavier, closer, and stronger plant can be used than could be tolerated for the wrapper leaf.

It is the custom in this part of the State to make two main crops of

PLATE III.

CHARACTERISTIC GROWTH OF HAMMOCK LAND AT FORT MEADE.

tobacco a year, namely, a spring crop and a fall crop. It is also customary to secure one or two sucker crops; that is, after the main crop is harvested a second crop is allowed to grow, and, as the plant has a full root development to nourish this sucker crop from the very start, the growth is rapid and usually rank and the leaves are strong and well fitted for filler purposes.

A plant intended for filler tobacco should be topped lower than one intended for wrapper leaves, so that the substance gathered by the roots will have fewer leaves to supply. The leaves will thus be stronger and more highly flavored. In the curing, also, the treatment of the wrapper and filler leaf is very different. The fermentation is carried much further with the filler, and petuning is practiced to still further increase the strength as well as to improve the aroma of the filler leaf.

It would unquestionably be well to specialize to a certain extent in the production of wrapper and filler leaves, and this is being done.

So far as it is safe to judge from a single season's experience, the high pine lands will grow a very pretty wrapper. The conditions are favorable for an even, rapid, and tender growth, as is apparent in the production of the truck crops. The conditions in these soils seem particularly well adapted to the production of a thin, elastic wrapper leaf. The best fillers, on the other hand, which have been produced so far have come from the hammock lands. At the same time the hammock soils have produced a very fine quality of wrapper leaf.

In order to secure the crop against injury from drought a very thorough system of irrigation is being practiced on the hammock lands. It is claimed that the crop matures in from forty-five to fifty days under judicious irrigation, against sixty to seventy days without irrigation. It is also claimed that it makes finer wrapper leaf.

The irrigation outfit consists of an engine placed near a watercourse, with a capacity of about 1 horsepower per acre and 1-inch or 1½-inch iron pipe laid near the surface of the ground for mains and laterals, the laterals being about 100 feet apart, with hydrants every 50 feet. Tanks are frequently used, but it is considered preferable now to pump directly into the mains so as to insure sufficient pressure. Nozzles are used which give an even spray, and which are moved from hydrant to hydrant by an attendant as the work progresses. Such an irrigation plant for a field of 20 acres or over costs from $100 to $150 per acre. Where the hydrants are not sufficiently close to cover the ground with spray a hose is used with a movable spray to water the space between the laterals. Plate IV shows the method of irrigation as practiced at Fort Meade.

Very recently the method of shading, which has been used with great success in the pineapple fields, has been adopted in connection with the tobacco. During the past season some very fine wrapper leaf was produced under the half shade at various places in the State. This method consists of erecting supports at convenient distances to carry a lattice formed of 3-inch strips placed 3 inches apart so that never more than half of the direct sun's rays reach the plant. This unquestionably maintains a more uniform condition of soil moisture and of relative humidity of air than is maintained in the open field. It insures a more continuous growth with less drain upon the plant during the heat of the day, and much more uniform conditions of growth at all times. These shades cost from $400 to $500 per acre. In some instances they have been completely covered with plant-bed muslin, so that the plants are never exposed to the intense rays of the sun.

It must not be forgotten that the tobacco plant when cut in the field is but the raw material out of which the finished product is to be made and with few of the properties of the finished leaf. Judgment must be exercised in setting out the plants, in the method of cultivation, in the matter of topping, and in the time of cutting. All of these are likely to have an important influence upon the plant grown upon any soil, but beyond this the barn curing, the fermentation, and the bale sweat must all be managed with the greatest care and judgment in order to bring out the fine qualities of the leaf. Each of these three processes is probably a distinct kind of fermentation, of the exact nature of which we have little certain knowledge. We know that it is necessary to maintain certain conditions in order that the leaf shall be in the proper condition for the changes which have to take place, although we do not know what these changes are nor the exact conditions which control them.

Even after the fermentation is apparently finished and the leaf put into the bale it should be allowed to remain undisturbed for at least two years in order to mellow with age and lose the harsh characteristics it still has when it comes out of the bulk. This is a matter of very great importance and one which can not be dwelt upon too strongly. The Florida grower has been too anxious to secure recognition for the crop, and has been compelled from lack of capital to sell his product immediately after it has been put into the bale. For this reason much of the tobacco has been made up into cigars without undergoing the bale sweat and, while much of the tobacco has given promise of good qualities, the full value of these has not been brought out for lack of age. This has done much harm to the tobacco industry of the State.

ETONIA SCRUB LANDS.

The great Etonia scrub formation was examined at Altoona. It is an impressive sight to stand at the border line between the scrub and the high pine land and notice the difference in the character of the vegetation. The high pine land is open, the trees are large and vigorous, and the ground is covered with a crop of grass which gives very good grazing for cattle. The vegetation is quick and generous and the most tender garden plants will grow luxuriantly if properly attended

PLATE IV.

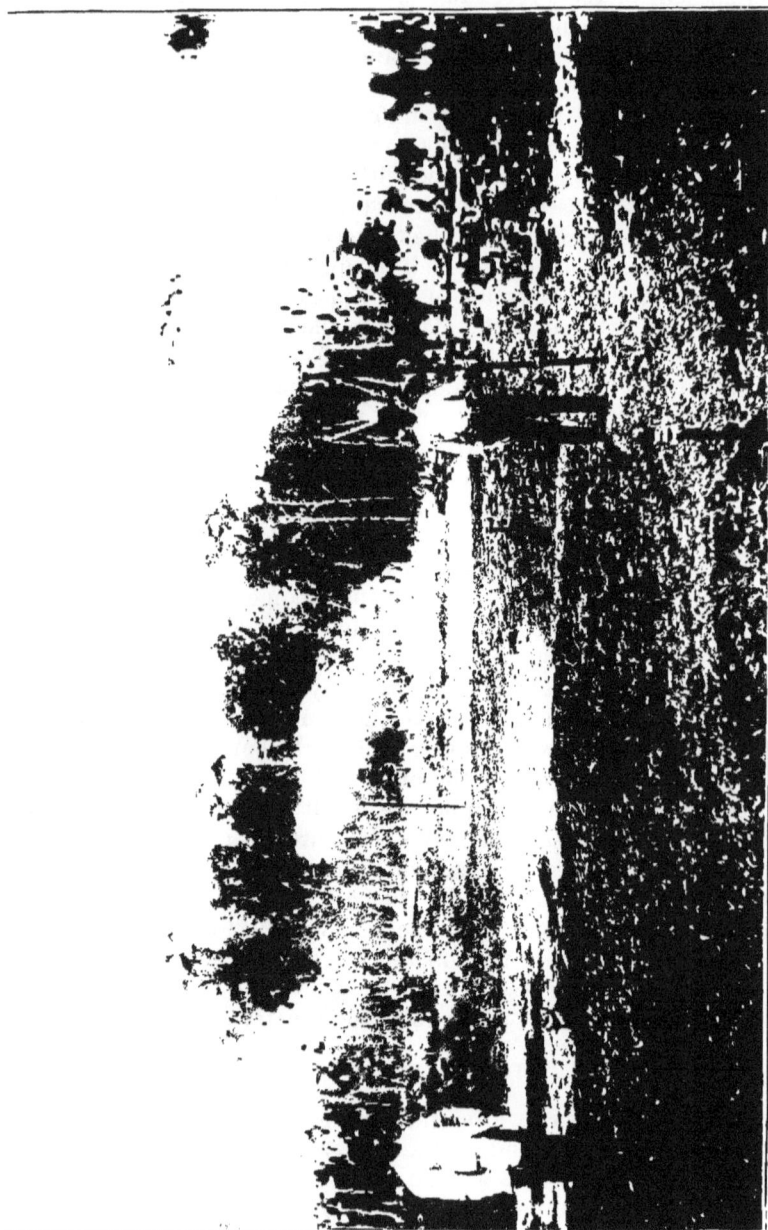

METHOD OF IRRIGATING TOBACCO LAND AT FORT MEADE.

15

to. These conditions stop abruptly at the edge of the scrub. The boundary between the high pine land and the scrub can be located without trouble within a few feet. Plate V shows the marked contrast between the vegetation of the scrub and the high pine lands, and shows also how abrupt the transition is from one kind of vegetation to the other.

In the scrub there is a dense growth of scrub oaks and low bushes and plants, all having thick leaves protected to the utmost from loss of water by evaporation by the property that desert plants have of turning the leaves up edgeways to the sun to expose as little surface as possible to the direct rays. No grass is found, and only the most hardy desert plants grow. When pines grow it is the dwarf spruce pine and not the long-leaf pine, while on the other hand the spruce pine is not found across the border in the high pine lands proper.

The full-grown scrub vegetation reaches about the height of a man's head, as can be seen in the illustration, Plate VI. This scrub growth stretches out at this place in an unbroken line for 10 or 15 miles to the northward, and the whole country presents a most desolate appearance. The country is generally rolling in both the high pine land and scrub. There are lakes at which the scrub and the high pine vegetation meet at the water's edge. There is no indication from the topography of the country of any difference in the climate over the two soils. Very few attempts are known to have been made to cultivate the scrub lands. A few efforts to grow truck and oranges are known to have been failures. It is generally believed that the scrub is colder at night and that frosts are liable to occur over these areas when they do not occur over the high pine land. There is no apparent reason for this, however, in the topography of the country. There are differences in elevation in the scrub, in quite short distances, of 25 feet or more, over which the same growth extends in an unbroken line following the contours of the surface. The same character of growth extends down to the lake borders in what is almost a muck soil.

It will be shown later that there is no apparent reason, from the chemical or physical examination, to account for this difference in the native growth on the scrub as compared with the high pine land or the hammock and, so far as our investigations show, there is no difference in the soil. The only explanation for the difference in the character of the vegetation is that it is accidental and that the one kind of crop or the other received a start and simply spread, the two kinds of vegetation not being capable of growing together. As a matter of fact, however, in comparing the scrub with the high pine land the conditions in the scrub appear more natural than those in the high pine land. In such sandy soils as these the wonder is that tender vegetables can be grown at all, and that such a large and generous growth of pines and grass is naturally produced.

PINEAPPLE LAND.

Pineapples are grown very extensively on the high pine land at Orlando, Winterhaven, and at many other places in the center of the peninsula, but along the east coast from Fort Pierce down to Lake Worth there is a narrow strip of country devoted almost entirely to the pineapple industry. The pineapple lands comprise here a narrow strip, hardly more than an eighth or a fourth of a mile wide with the Indian River or the ocean on one side and the pine flats on the other, stretching out into the great savannas or everglades. The ridge has an average elevation of perhaps 15 or 20 feet. The growth is mainly scrub oak, spruce pine, and palmetto. Much of it is quite dense and the character of the growth makes it quite expensive to clear the land. The soil is a coarse sand, almost pure white and to all appearance as free from any trace of plant food as the cleanest glass sand. The subsoil is either a coarse white or yellow sand. The yellow sand is generally preferred, as it is considered rather stronger than the white. Nothing would seem more unpromising to a Northern farmer than the white sand thrown out from a ditch or exposed in a railroad cut extending through these pineapple soils, upon which the pineapple industry is so profitable and the returns are so sure that the growers can not only afford enormous applications of fertilizers, but expend from $400 to $500 an acre in irrigation or in covering the fields with open lattice sheds.

Until within the last year or two there was a lack of transportation facilities in this section. Owing to this, no truck crops or oranges had been grown except for family use. It is considered that the soils are too dry for trucking without excessive fertilization and watering, which could probably not be economically done. At Jensen and at Eden the country along the railroad looks like a continuous field of pineapples.

This land presents some very interesting problems to the student of the soil, as it appears to be lacking in every requisite of food and to have the physical conditions most unsuited to agricultural purposes. Having said so much, it may not be out of place to give an idea of the relative value of these lands for this special crop. This may be gathered from the following statement of the cost of starting a pineapple plantation at the present time at West Palmbeach.

The land costs uncleared from $50 to $100 an acre, or, if it is on the lake front, as much as $200 per acre. Clearing the land will cost from $75 to $100 per acre. It will require from 10,000 to 12,000 pineapple slips to set the acre, 18 by 18, or 20 by 20 inches between the plants. The common Red Spanish variety costs $5 per thousand, or $60 per acre. The fancy kinds of pineapple which are being set out now cost from $10 to $25 per hundred. Setting out the slips costs about $20 per acre. The slips are usually set out in July or August, and bear the first crop in a year from the following April, that is, in about twenty

Plate VI.

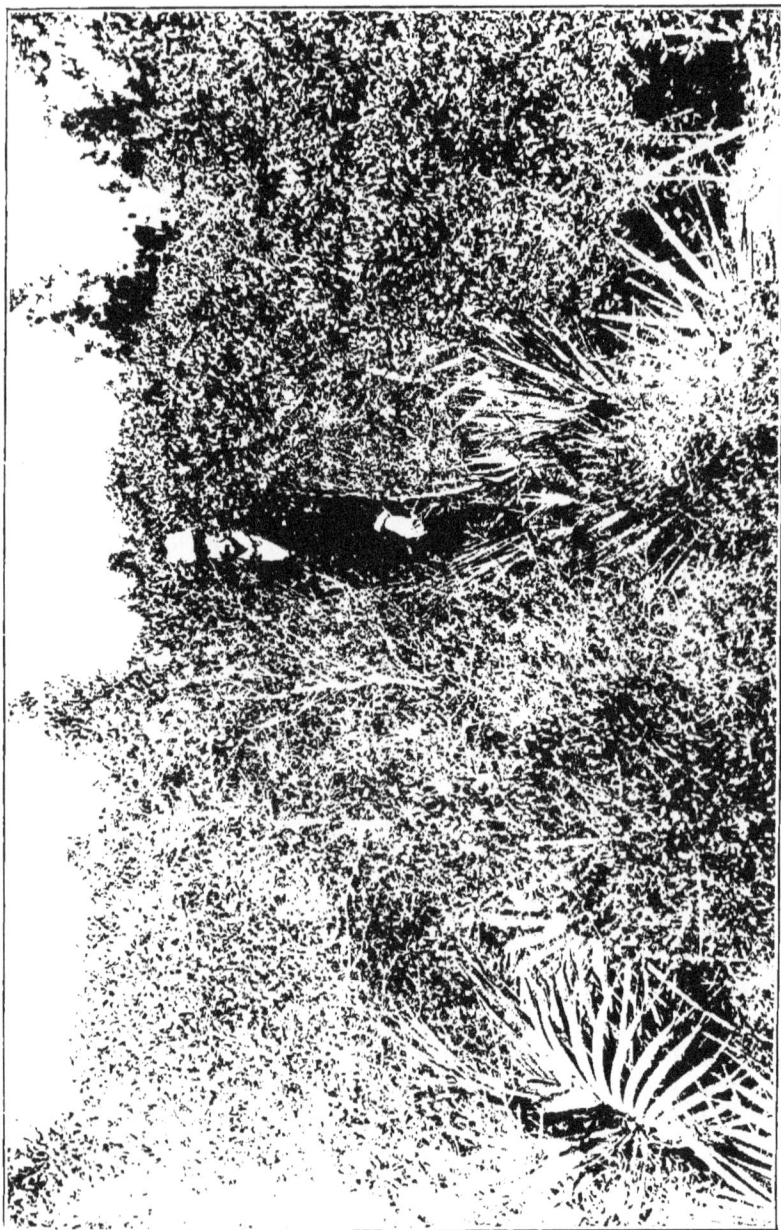

Characteristic Growth of Etonia Scrub at Altoona.

or twenty-two months from the time of setting out. One and a half to 2 tons of fertilizers are used per acre, applied in portions two or three times during the season. The more fertilizer used the more the crop is benefited. The crop responds generously to each application. Cotton seed, cotton-seed hulls, tobacco stems, and sulphate of potash are commonly used and cost from $40 to $60 per acre. Irrigation has been tried on rather an extensive scale and latterly shading has come into considerable use. The shading costs from $450 to $500 per acre, depending upon the distance from the sawmills. Only the finest varieties of pineapples, however, are shaded at present.

There is no more striking example of the adaptation of special soil conditions to particular crops than is afforded here, and the utilizing of conditions which could not possibly have been used for general agricultural purposes. If the whole country were looked over it would be hard to find a less promising soil than this, which, however, through a peculiar adaptation to a certain kind of plant has, when cleared and planted, a value ranging from $500 to $2,500 per acre and even more.

The months of March, April, and May constitute the dry season for that locality, and the two latter months are important in the pineapple industry, as that is the time when the apple is forming. Serious damage has often been done at this season by severe droughts, and to provide against this injury irrigation has been employed to quite a considerable extent. The usual method of irrigation is to produce a fine overhead spray with standpipes 3 or 4 feet high at intervals of from 15 or 20 feet each way. This method has not been altogether satisfactory, however, and lately the method of shading has come into considerable use. The roof of the open shed consists of 3-inch strips nailed to light frame work, the strips being 3 inches apart, so that less than one-half as much sunlight falls upon the plants or the surface of the ground as would be received if the shed were not there. This tends to retard evaporation from the soil and from the plant. It is also very efficient in protecting the plants against frosts, and it is used for this purpose extensively in the northern part of the pineapple area.

LAFAYETTE FORMATION OF WESTERN FLORIDA.

The Lafayette formation in western Florida is a continuation southward of the "red lands" of Wedgefield and Aiken, South Carolina, and of Georgia. It constitutes the oldest tobacco area of the State, where a fine quality of tobacco was grown many years ago and where the industry was first taken up again in the recent developments in the State. The tobacco industry was revived at Quincy about ten years ago in the introduction of cigar tobacco.

The soil of this locality is a fine, light, sandy loam, resting upon what appears to be a strong clay subsoil of considerable depth. The loam is generally from 6 to 18 inches deep, but the red clay is frequently

18335—No. 13——2

exposed in road cuts and washed places in the fields. The country is rolling and covered with a native vegetation of hard wood trees.

It will be seen from the table of mechanical analyses that the loam overlying the red-clay subsoil contains about 5 per cent of clay. It corresponds closely with the tobacco soils of the Connecticut Valley and the early truck soils of the Atlantic coast States. It is advisable to have a depth of at least 12 or 18 inches of this loam over the clay for the production of a fine grade of wrapper leaf.

It will be seen from the table of mechanical analyses that the red-clay subsoil of these lands contains upward of 30 per cent of clay, fully as much as the heavy limestone soils of Pennsylvania and Ohio. There is, however, this peculiarity in this "red-land" formation as it occurs here and in South Carolina—that is, that it maintains only about 8 or 10 per cent of water, while soils having the same percentage of clay in Pennsylvania and Ohio on which a similar leaf is produced contain as much as from 18 to 22 per cent of water. A few records were obtained of the water content of the soil at Quincy and it was found to maintain about 8 per cent of water on the average to a depth of 24 inches. Strangely enough this is about the same percentage as is maintained by the hammock soil at Fort Meade, although the soils are so very different in their texture and general appearance. It is curious that the light sandy soils of the hammock land maintain so much water as this, and it is likewise singular that so little water is maintained on the average by these Lafayette clays which have so much real clay in their composition. Very little difference is shown to exist, therefore, between the tobacco soil of Quincy and the hammock soil at Fort Meade in regard to the water content or, as will be shown presently, in the soluble salt content of the lands. The statements in regard to the tobacco industry at Fort Meade apply equally to this section.

COMPARISON OF THE PRINCIPAL TYPES OF FLORIDA SOIL.

TEXTURE OF THE SOILS.

It will be seen from the brief description which has been given of the principal types examined that there is a marked difference in the character of the growth and in the agricultural value of the lands. The object of the present investigation has been to see if there is any reason to explain these differences. The problem was to discover, if possible, why the hammock land maintains a growth of oak, hickory, dogwood, and other hard-wood trees, often so overgrown with a luxuriant growth of bushes and vines as to make an impenetrable jungle. The pine lands, on the other hand, have no hard-wood trees except occasional scrub oaks, but support a vigorous growth of pine trees, with a luxuriant crop of grass and but scant undergrowth. The Lafayette formation has a characteristic hard wood growth. It has a subsoil containing far more clay than any other formation in Florida, and yet it has about the same agricultural value as the hammock soil at Fort Meade. The scrub land has a characteristic growth of scrub oaks and dwarf bushes, two peculiar species of palmetto, and the spruce pine.

The following tables give the mean texture as determined from the mechanical analyses of a number of samples of soil and subsoil from the various formations in the State, the detailed analyses upon which these are based being given at the end of this bulletin:

Summary of the mechanical analyses of Florida lands.

SOILS.

Number of samples.	Kind of land.	Organic matter.	Gravel (2–1 mm.).	Coarse sand (1–0.5 mm.).	Medium sand (0.5–0.25 mm.).	Fine sand (0.25–0.1 mm.).	Very fine sand (0.1–0.05 mm.).	Silt (0.05–0.01 mm.).	Fine silt (0.01–0.005 mm.).	Clay (0.005–0.0001 mm.).
		Per ct.	Per ct.	Per ct.	Per ct.	Per ct.	Per ct.	Per ct.	Per ct.	Per ct.
2	Spruce pine scrub ...	1.06	0.65	12.36	41.42	41.18	2.40	0.16	0.06	0.35
4	Pineapple land	1.21	.23	3.02	61.11	33.76	.54	.22	.06	.50
4	Etonia scrub........	1.24	.23	3.34	27.43	58.60	7.60	.55	.20	.87
12	High pine land	1.82	1.46	5.78	23.89	45.11	18.42	.96	.38	1.56
5	Gray hammock	1.84	.36	3.29	19.75	52.17	19.08	.66	.50	1.68
4	Light hammock......	1.38	Trace.	3.63	28.85	51.37	10.34	1.38	.62	1.70
4	Rich, heavy hammock	2.68	.82	2.48	19.60	44.15	19.07	3.35	1.19	4.48
4	Mixed land..........	2.00	.05	2.91	26.65	49.17	10.66	2.05	.74	4.75
4	Lafayette...........	2.68	.68	4.85	20.03	45.53	14.93	4.15	.80	5.15

SUBSOILS.

1	Spruce pine land.....	0.45	0.66	9.07	32.58	52.13	3.26	0.23	0.18	0.51
5	Pineapple land	.31	.06	3.08	57.50	37.78	.59	.07	.13	.52
4	Gray hammock	1.61	.27	3.79	22.99	53.53	14.54	.48	.30	1.22
4	Etonia scrub........	.56	.24	3.49	29.64	57.47	5.85	.74	.22	1.56
12	High pine land	.84	1.51	5.72	23.29	47.51	17.61	.87	.34	1.87
6	Light hammock	.71	.15	3.72	28.10	53.79	8.97	1.30	.59	2.07
5	Mixed land	1.25	.06	2.62	22.05	53.55	10.99	1.79	.80	5.66
6	Rich, heavy hammock	3.97	.91	2.74	13.37	29.32	13.19	7.31	2.52	22.82
4	Lafayette...........	5.69	.54	1.94	8.81	35.15	13.39	3.37	1.07	29.30

The samples are arranged in the table according to the percentage of clay they contain, the least first. Leaving out of account for the moment the last three formations, which constitute a relatively small area of the peninsula proper, the other six formations, representing the important types of agricultural land supporting very different kinds of native vegetation, differ in their texture hardly more than the limit of error in the mechanical analysis. The analyses are so nearly alike that it would not be safe to consider the differences shown in the table as indicating any real difference in the texture.

In the soils of the Atlantic seaboard generally the relations of the soils to water depend mainly upon the amount of clay present in the soil. The relation of the soils to native vegetation and agricultural crops depends likewise indirectly upon the amount of clay they contain, as this determines largely the amount of water they maintain. The pine lands and the truck lands have, as a rule, not over 5 or 10 per cent of clay, while the oak and hickory soils contain not less than 20 per cent. In these Florida types, however, there is hardly more than 2 per cent of silt, fine silt, and clay all put together. The bulk of the soil consists of the two grades of medium and fine sand, but the proportion of these two grades seems to bear no relation whatever to the difference in the agricultural value of the lands.

The pineapple lands of the east coast consist of a pure white sand, with rather more of the medium grade and rather less of the grade of fine sand. With this exception there is little or no difference in the texture of the pineapple land, the gray hammock, the Etonia scrub, the high pine land, or the light hammock. There is probably no greater difference in the native vegetation of any two soils of the United States than in the gray hammock and the Etonia scrub, and yet they are seen to have the same texture, and it will appear later that they have the same chemical composition. No difference has been found, therefore, in the texture of these soils which will explain in any way the difference in their agricultural value. The rich, heavy hammock, underlaid with marl, the mixed land from the neighborhood of Ocala, and the Lafayette formation from the western part of the State differ from the other six formations principally in the amount of clay they contain.

CHEMICAL COMPOSITION OF THE SOILS.

The following table, giving the mean chemical composition of a number of Florida soils as regards several of the important plant foods, has been compiled from Bulletin No. 43 of the Florida Experiment Station:

Average chemical composition of Florida soils and subsoils.

	Hilgard's average of soils.	Florida soils.		
		Soils.	Subsoils.	Mean of all.
	Per cent.	Per cent.	Per cent.	Per cent.
Potash, K₂O	0.216	0.009	0.004	0.007
Lime, CaO	.108	.072	.021	.051
Phosphoric acid, P₂O₅	.113	.071	.065	.069
Magnesia, MgO	.225	.031	.019	.026
Nitrogen, N		.052	.011	.035

There are thirty-four soils and twenty-three subsoils represented, while the last column gives the mean of the whole number of fifty-seven samples. The types of soils are not clearly stated in the text of the bulletin, but the samples selected represent as far as possible both the hammock and the high pine land. For comparison, Hilgard's averages for 466 soils of the humid portion of the United States are given in the first column.[1]

Hilgard states elsewhere that soils containing less than 0.1 of 1 per cent of either potash, lime, or phosphoric acid may be regarded as having a deficiency of that particular substance.

[1] Bulletin No. 3 of the United States Weather Bureau, a Report on the Relations of Soils to Climate, p. 30.

It will be seen that the food content of these Florida soils is exceedingly low. The average potash content is less than 0.01 of 1 per cent. The amounts of lime, phosphoric acid, magnesia, and nitrogen are so low that it seems almost inconceivable that such soils support such a luxuriant growth of native vegetation and are so extremely productive of the crops adapted to the climate and soil conditions. It is remarkable that soils containing so little plant food should support the vegetation found on these Florida lands.

Composite samples of five of the typical soil formations from the collection of the Department of Agriculture, and consisting in each case of from four to ten samples, were analyzed in the Division of Chemistry, with the results given in the accompanying table.

Chemical analyses of composite samples of Florida soils.

Soils.	K_2O.	CaO.	MgO.	P_2O_5.	N.
	Per cent.	*Per cent.*	*Per cent.*	*Per cent.*	*Per cent.*
Pineapple land	0.005	0.025	0.009	0.005	0.028
Etonia scrub	.003	.030	.013	.008	.028
High pine land	.007	.060	.020	.110	.028
Light hammock	.015	.090	.040	.090	.042
Gray hammock	.009	.090	.036	.320	.042

These results show again the very small amount of plant food contained in these Florida soils. There is no difference in the chemical composition, as shown by the results of this work, which would account in any way for the difference in the native vegetation of these soils. One would not think of selecting any one of these soils from a table of analyses as adapted to the growth of hard wood trees or to oranges, tobacco, or even to truck crops.

SOLUBLE SALT CONTENT OF SOILS.

Although the analyses show a remarkably small percentage of the mineral plant foods in these soils, really within the limit of error of chemical analyses, still, on account of the enormous weight of the soils per acre, there is a very considerable amount of food material actually at the disposal of the plants. If these sandy soils are estimated to weigh 4,000,000 pounds per acre to a depth of 1 foot, there would be about 6,000 pounds per acre of potash, phosphoric acid, and lime. Calculated on the same basis, from the figures in the first column of Table 3, there is about 26,000 pounds of these plant foods present on the average in the soils of the humid regions of the United States. These figures represent the total amount of these plant foods soluble in strong hydrochloric acid. An investigation was made to determine how much of this food material was actually present in solution in the soil moisture. The determinations were made by the electrical method described in Bulletin No. 8 of this division. The results are given in the accompanying table.

Soluble salt content of Florida soils.

No.	Locality.	Soils.	In 100 grams.		In 1 acre.[1]	
			Soil.	Subsoil.	Soil.	Subsoil.
			Mg.	*Mg.*	*Pounds.*	*Pounds.*
2886	West Palmbeach	Pineapple land	0.90	0.34	36	13
2871	Winterhaven	Truck, high pine land	1.56	.80	62	32
2869	Grand Island	....do	2.09	1.04	84	42
2915	Altoona	Scrub	.95	.94	37	38
2857	Rockledge	Orange, gray hammock	2.10	1.00	84	40
2824	Fort Meade	High pine land (first quality)	1.14		46	
2817	....do	Tobacco, heavy hammock	1.16	1.36	46	54
2826	....do	High pine land (third quality)	1.08	1.27	43	51
2894	Quincy	Lafayette, tobacco		1.88		75

[1] Estimated to a depth of 1 foot on a basis of 4,000,000 pounds of soil per acre for this depth.

It will be seen that in no case does the amount of soluble salts present in the soil approach 100 pounds per acre to a depth of 12 inches. The hammock land at Fort Meade contains, to a depth of 1 foot, approximately only 46 pounds of mineral salts of all kinds dissolved in the soil moisture, and yet this soil produces naturally a heavy growth of hard wood trees, and is considered one of the finest soils for oranges, tobacco, truck, and similar quick-growing and exhausting crops. There is no difference in the soluble salt content, as determined by this electrical method, which would account in any way for the great difference in the native vegetation of these soils.

The chemical analyses show not only that there is a very small amount of plant food present in the soil, but these figures indicate that only about 1 per cent of this is present in a soluble form. The results so far obtained in this division indicate that the average soils of the Northern States contain upward of 1,000 pounds of mineral salts dissolved in the soil moisture, and this is approximately 5 per cent of the amount of mineral matter present soluble in strong hydrochloric acid.

These results all seem to show that these types of Florida soil constitute a distinct class of soils, unlike the average soils of the humid portions of the United States. There is no difference in the physical texture, the chemical composition, or the soluble salt content to explain the wonderful fertility and the difference in the character of the native vegetation, and one must look to other properties than those generally recognized by agricultural investigators for causes which will explain the facts. The following investigations on the relation of these soils to moisture offer a partial explanation.

MOISTURE CONTENT OF FLORIDA SOILS.

It has already been noticed that the soils of the high pine lands maintain a very uniform amount of moisture, even in seasons of protracted drought. Moisture determinations were made in the truck land at Winterhaven. Fla., during the season of 1897, with the results given in the accompanying table.

The moisture content of high pine truck land, 3 to 6 inches deep, at Winterhaven, Fla.

[Moisture determined by the electrical method.]

Day of month.	April. Moisture.	April. Rain.	May. Moisture.	May. Rain.	June. Moisture.	June. Rain.	July. Moisture.	July. Rain.
	Per cent.	Inches.	Per cent.	Inches.	Per cent.	Inches.	Per cent.	Inches.
1	6.85	....	5.47	0.10	4.15	....	3.36	0.10
2	6.04	....	4.72	....	4.19	....	3.55	....
3	6.01	....	4.29	....	5.13	0.31	3.44	2.95
4	5.90	....	4.27	....	4.51	.18	3.34	....
5	4.53	....	4.31	....	4.15	.05	3.34	....
6	5.85	0.30	4.51	....	3.97	....	3.34	....
7	5.82	....	4.11	....	....	....	3.44	.30
8	9.59	....	4.11	....	....	....	3.63	....
9	6.72	1.80	4.11	....	....	....	3.55	.30
10	5.51	.02	4.10	....	....	....	4.15	1.35
11	5.49	....	4.06	....	4.44	....	3.44	....
12	4.99	....	4.07	.10	4.15	....	3.97	1.43
13	4.82	....	9.28	2.10	3.82	....	3.55	....
14	4.89	....	5.13	....	3.63	....	3.54	....
15	....	....	4.54	....	3.82	.23	3.44	....
16	4.85	....	4.48	....	4.31	.58	3.54	....
17	4.64	....	4.73	....	3.97	.02	3.55	.10
18	4.31	....	4.84	....	3.76	....	3.44	....
19	4.27	....	4.49	....	3.55	....	3.55	....
20	4.21	....	4.42	....	3.55	....	3.44	....
21	4.06	....	4.35	....	13.79	.05	3.55	.47
22	4.05	....	4.40	....	4.81	.90	3.44	....
23	4.06	....	4.35	....	3.97	....	3.55	....
24	4.04	....	4.59	....	3.68	.10	3.55	.13
25	4.01	....	4.15	....	3.55	....	3.68	.92
26	4.04	....	4.31	....	3.68	.13	3.44	.25
27	4.04	....	4.27	....	3.51	....	3.68	....
28	4.06	....	4.27	....	3.68	....	3.55	....
29	4.03	....	4.29	....	3.48	....	3.55	.23
30	5.24	.70	4.23	.15	3.55	....	3.68	.35
31	....	....	4.23	....	....	....	3.55	.82
Mean	5.06	2.82	4.56	2.48	3.95	3.45	3.54	10.00

Four and a half per cent of water appears to be an abundant supply for the vegetables on these soils. Six per cent of moisture makes the soil quite wet. There were periods of two or three weeks without rain, and yet the moisture supply never fell below 3 per cent during the time of the observations. Furthermore, it is rather strange to note that during what is considered the dry season of April and May, with only two or three rains of any magnitude, the moisture in the soil was considerably higher than during June and July, when the rains were both heavy and frequent. This is in line with the general experience of the farmers. The moisture supply is seen to be very uniform. The effect of a rain of even 1 or 2 inches is hardly appreciable twenty-four hours after the rain has ceased. The excess of water seems to drain away very rapidly. Owing to this fact the rainfalls, where they occur in the table, seem to affect the moisture content of the soils very differently. This is owing to the difference in the time between the cessation of the rain and the taking of the observations. No reason can be assigned for the peculiar property these soils possess which enables them to maintain so uniform a water content. There were no crops growing on the soil at the time these observations were taken, so that no special demands were made upon the moisture except as a result of evaporaation from the surface.

Records were also kept, by the electrical method, of the moisture content of the hammock soils at Fort Meade at a depth of from 3 to 6 inches. The results are given in the accompanying table.

The moisture content of hammock tobacco soil, 3 to 6 inches deep, at Fort Meade, Fla.

[Moisture determined by the electrical method.]

Day of month.	April.		May.		June.		July.	
	Moisture.	Rain.	Moisture.	Rain.	Moisture.	Rain.	Moisture.	Rain.
	Per cent.	*Inches.*	*Per cent.*	*Inches.*	*Per cent.*	*Inches.*	*Per cent.*	*Inches.*
1	5.21	0.07	10.20	0.12			7.94	
2	5.35		10.31				7.48	0.28
3	5.32		8.32				10.53	1.32
4	5.35		7.80				8.95	
5	5.56	0.60	7.56				10.71	0.41
6		0.86	7.33				9.26	8.04
7	10.76	0.20	7.05		7.48	0.13	9.24	
8	9.58		7.09		7.45	0.55	9.22	0.15
9	13.06	0.93	7.02		7.96		10.09	0.11
10	10.31	0.30	6.77		9.05		9.21	0.07
11	9.42		6.80		7.91		10.49	0.47
12	9.30		13.63	1.30	8.06		11.00	1.96
13	9.28		11.37	1.90	7.96		10.76	1.89
14	9.13		9.24	0.30	10.83	0.59	9.66	0.14
15	8.94		11.00	1.05	8.62	0.67	8.40	
16	8.81		9.74		9.04	0.03	9.45	0.08
17	8.54				8.85		8.06	
18	8.38				7.78		8.72	0.19
19	8.06		8.23		8.16	0.17	8.51	
20	8.01		8.02		8.57	0.19	8.06	
21	7.69		7.87		8.82	0.47	7.87	
22	7.74		7.87		8.54		9.06	0.24
23	7.74		7.78		9.05		8.72	
24	7.61				8.72		8.43	
25	7.56				8.85	0.41	10.62	0.82
26	6.89				8.98		10.74	
27	6.74				8.95	0.36	8.72	
28	6.69				8.67		8.80	
29	6.60				7.45		8.12	
30	10.82	0.77			7.93		8.85	0.32
31							8.98	0.18
Mean.	7.76	3.63	[1] 8.62	[1] 4.67	[1] 8.49	[1] 3.57	9.20	8.67

[1] Excluding a period of fourteen days in May and June, during which it is not known whether rain fell or not.

It will be noticed that this hammock soil contains on an average between 8 and 9 per cent of moisture, or nearly twice as much as the truck soil at Winterhaven. Furthermore, the evaporation is very much greater and the crops suffer quicker from drought than on the high pine land. No reason can be given why such a light sandy soil as the hammock soil at Fort Meade should maintain as much as 8 per cent of water. The soils are deep and well drained, and they contain, as has been already shown, very little clay, yet the moisture content is as great as in the red lands at Quincy, Fla., which are underlaid with subsoils containing upward of 30 per cent of clay. This is a matter which needs very thorough investigation, and the very striking difference in the relation of these two types of soil to moisture will undoubtedly explain in large part the difference in the character of the native growth and in the agricultural value of the soils. It remains to be shown, also, why as little as 8 per cent of water is amply sufficient for a growth of oaks and other hard wood trees on these sandy soils of Florida, while at least 15 or 20 per cent of water is necessary for oaks and similar hard wood trees on the soils at the North. The accompanying diagram (fig. 1) shows clearly the difference in the water content of these two kinds of Florida soil.

Records were kept of the moisture content of the pineapple land at West Palmbeach in the open field and under the half shade, which is used there so successfully. The determinations were made by the old tube method, and represent the moisture content in the top foot of soil. During the dry months of April and May the soil under the shed contains, as a rule, about twice as much water as the soil in the open field. This is unquestionably an important matter at this critical time in the development of the crop. During the months of June and July, when there was an abundance of rain, there was little or no difference between the water content of the field and under the shed. The influence of the half shade in protecting the soil from loss of water during the time of protracted drought is of the utmost importance and should be more

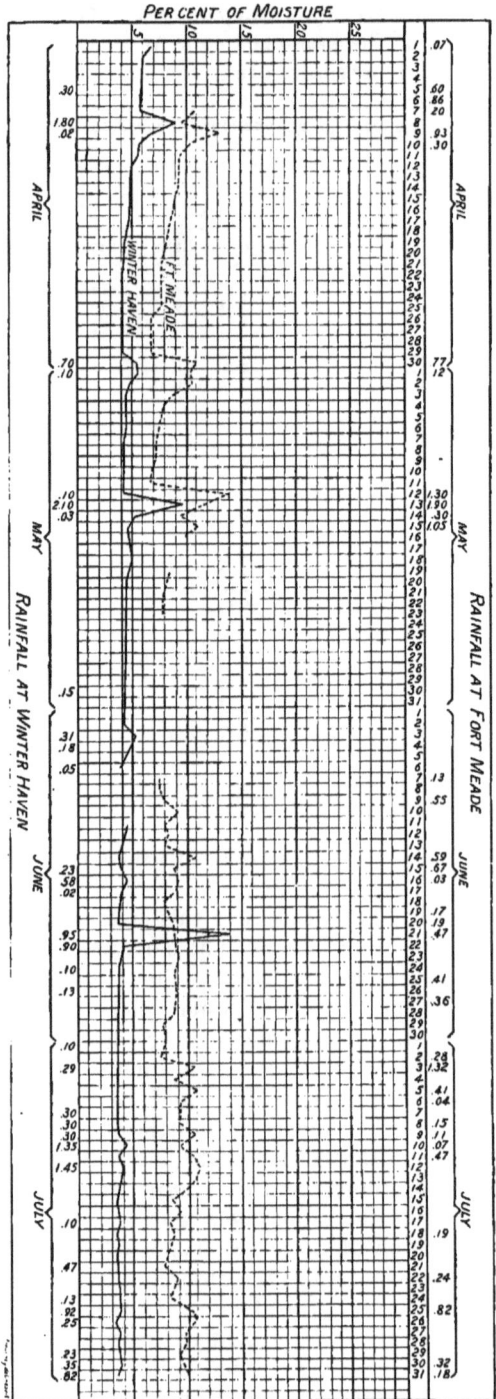

Fig. 1.—Diagram showing moisture content of the hammock soils at Fort Meade and high pine soil at Winterhaven.

fully investigated, and records should be kept with the electrical method, which will give more reliable results, and the observations should be continued over several seasons in various kinds of soil. The accompanying table gives the data obtained from these records and the accompanying diagrams show graphically the difference in the water content of the soils during the dry period and the wet season. (Figs. 2 and 3.)

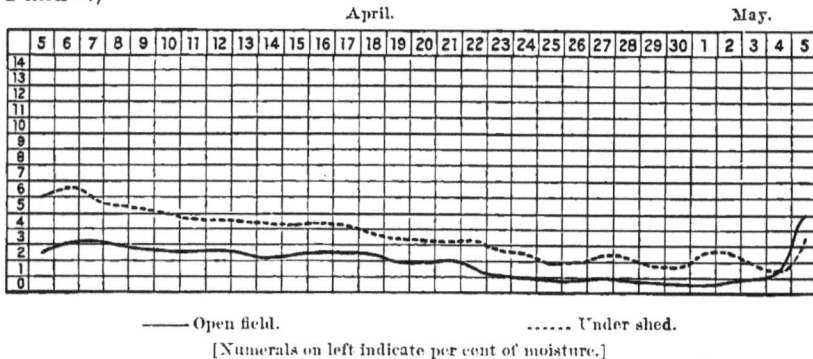

FIG. 2.—Diagram showing influence of half shading in conserving moisture in pineapple land at West Palmbeach, Fla., during dry season. Showers are reported on April 17, 18, 21, May 3, 4, 5—amount not stated.

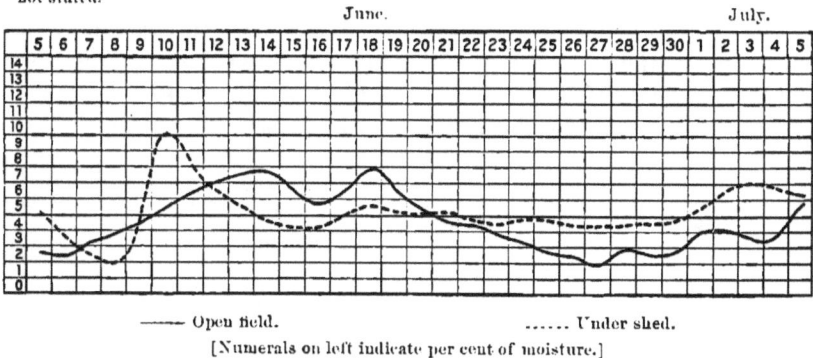

FIG. 3.—Diagram illustrating conditions in pineapple land in open field and under half shade at West Palmbeach, Fla., during rainy season. Pineapples ripening and being shipped.

Pineapple land at West Palmbeach, Fla., 1896.

Day.	April.			May.			June.			July.		
	Field.	Shed.	Weather.	Field.	Shed.	Weather.	Field.	Shed.	Weather.	Field.	Shed.	Weather.
	Per ct.	Per ct.		Per ct.	Per ct.		Per ct.	Per ct.		Per ct.	Per ct.	
1	....	....	....	0.6	2.5	....	0.5	0.4	....	4.0	5.4	
2	....	....	Rain..	.8	2.5	....	1.2	.1	....	4.0	6.5	
3	....	....	....	1.0	1.8	....	6.0	4.0	Rain..	3.5	7.0	Rain.
4	....	....	....	1.5	1.5	Rain..	4.0	5.4	Rain..	3.6	6.6	
5	2.5	6.0	....	5.0	3.4	Rain..	2.5	5.2	Rain..	5.8	6.4	Rain.
6	3.0	6.5	....	4.0	6.5	Rain..	2.3	3.6	....	5.3	6.3	Rain.
7	3.2	6.0	....	3.0	6.4	Rain..	3.2	2.6	Rain..	5.1	6.8	
8	3.0	5.6	....	2.0	2.6	....	3.8	2.0	....	5.0	7.0	Rain.
9	2.8	5.3	....	1.5	1.8	....	4.6	4.0	Rain..	4.5	6.0	Rain.
10	2.5	5.0	....	1.3	1.8	....	5.5	10.0	Rain..	4.8	3.5	
11	2.5	4.8	....	1.5	3.0	....	6.4	8.0	....	3.0	2.0	Rain.
12	2.6	4.8	....	2.0	3.8	....	7.0	6.5	Rain..	2.6	1.2	
13	2.4	4.6	....	2.4	4.0	....	7.5	5.6	Rain..	2.0	1.2	
14	2.1	4.4	....	2.4	2.5	....	7.8	4.8	Rain..	2.0	1.8	
15	2.3	4.3	....	2.2	3.0	....	6.5	4.2	Rain..	2.1	2.4	

Pineapple land at West Palmbeach, Fla., 1896—Continued.

Day.	April.			May.			June.			July.		
	Field.	Shed.	Weather.	Field.	Shed.	Weather.	Field.	Shed.	Weather.	Field.	Shed.	Weather.
	Per ct.	Per ct.		Per ct.	Per ct.		Per ct.	Per ct.		Per ct.	Per ct.	
16	2.5	4.3		1.5	2.8		5.7	4.1		2.6	3.4	
17	2.5	4.2	Rain..	.8	3.0		6.5	5.0		3.6	4.4	
18	2.4	3.8	Rain..	.4	2.1		8.0	5.6		5.0	5.4	
19	2.0	3.5		.3	2.2		6.6	5.2		6.0	6.0	Rain..
20	2.0	3.3		.4	3.0		5.6	5.1		5.1	5.5	
21	2.1	3.2	Rain..	.6	2.8	Rain..	4.8	5.2		4.5	5.1	
22	1.5	3.2		1.0	2.6	Rain..	4.4	4.8		3.6	5.0	
23	1.1	2.9		1.3	2.6	Rain..	3.8	4.4		3.0	5.0	
24	1.0	2.5		1.8	2.2		3.3	4.8		2.5	5.1	
25	.9	2.0		2.4	1.8		2.7	4.8		2.0	5.2	
26	.9	2.0		2.1	1.8	Rain..	2.4	4.3		1.8	4.5	
27	1.0	2.2		2.0	1.6		1.9	4.3		1.6	3.5	
28	.8	2.1		1.8	1.5		2.8	4.3	Rain..	1.5	1.8	
29	.7	1.8		1.9	1.5	Rain..	2.4	4.4	Rain..	1.5	1.6	
30	.6	1.7		1.8	1.3	Rain..	2.8	4.7	Rain..	1.0	1.6	
31				1.1	1.8					1.0	1.4	
	2.0	3.8		1.7	2.6		4.4	4.6		3.3	4.3	

A series of moisture determinations were made in the scrub and the adjacent high pine land at Altoona for a period of two months during the season of 1896. The determinations were made by the old method of taking samples of the soil in small brass tubes and sending them, protected from evaporation, to the laboratory of the Department, where careful moisture determinations were made. The results of these daily observations were then platted and a curve drawn through the mean positions occupied by the actual points of observation. The mean daily readings, as thus deduced, are given in the accompanying table:

Water content of high pine and scrub land at Altoona, Fla., in 1896.

Day of month.	April.		May.	
	Pine land.	Scrub.	Pine land.	Scrub.
	Per cent.	Per cent.	Per cent.	Per cent.
1			4.2	4.5
2	4.7	5.8	3.8	3.6
3	4.0	5.0	3.4	2.9
4	3.3	4.1	3.0	2.4
5	2.9	3.5	2.6	2.0
6	2.4	2.9	2.3	1.7
7	2.0	2.4	2.0	1.4
8	1.4	1.9	1.8	1.1
9	7.0	6.8	1.5	1.0
10	4.9	5.5	1.3	.9
11	4.4	4.6	1.1	.8
12	4.0	4.1		
13	3.7	3.7		
14	3.4	3.2		
15	3.0	2.8		
16	2.7	2.5	3.3	3.8
17	2.5	2.1	3.1	3.3
18	2.2	1.9	2.9	2.8
19	2.1	1.5	2.7	2.4
20	1.9	1.3	2.6	2.0
21	1.8	2.5	2.4	1.7
22	1.6	2.1	2.3	1.5
23	1.5	1.9	2.1	1.3
24	1.4	1.6	2.0	1.1
25	1.3	1.4	1.9	.9
26	1.2	1.2	1.8	.8
27	1.1	1.0	1.7	.7
28	1.0	.9	1.6	.6
29	1.0	.8	1.5	.6
30	4.7	5.5	2.7	2.9
31			2.4	2.5
Mean	2.7	2.9	2.4	1.9

28

The records show that there is no apparent difference in the moisture content of these two soils during the dry season, and there is nothing here which suggests any difference in the water content of the soils to explain the difference in the relation of these soils to crops and to the native vegetation. The amount of water in each appears to be very small, but on the high pine lands the conditions are favorable for vigorous growth for the most tender vegetables. The native growth in the scrub, on the other hand, shows the main characteristics of desert plants and of arid conditions. With an apparently equal moisture supply, plants on one soil appear to get all the moisture they require, while the plants on the other soil, having the same texture and the same chemical composition, have all the appearance of having been grown under extremely arid conditions.

The following table gives the detailed results of the mechanical analyses of the Florida samples:

Mechanical analyses of soils and subsoils.

No.	Locality.	Description.	Moisture in air dry sample.	Organic matter.	Gravel (2-1 mm.).	Coarse sand (1-0.5 mm.).	Medium sand (0.5-0.25 mm.).	Finesand (0.25-1 mm.).	Very fine sand (0.1-0.05 mm.).	Silt (0.05-0.01 mm.).	Fine silt (0.01-0.005 mm.).	Clay (0.005-0.0001 mm.).
			P. ct.	*P. ct.*	*P. ct.*	*P. ct.*	*P. ct.*	*P. ct.*	*P. ct.*	*P. ct.*	*P. ct.*	*P. ct.*
2212	West Palm beach.	Pineapple land, 0"-6"	0.09	0.59	0.91	3.43	65.29	29.98	0.17	0.08	0.08	0.37
2890	....do	Pineapple land, 0"-6"	.11	.99	.00	2.30	57.12	38.52	.83	.13	.05	.40
2886	....do	Pineapple land, 0"-6"	.16	1.37	.00	4.03	65.79	27.55	.50	.50	.02	.52
2888	....do	Pineapple land, 0"-6"	.23	1.87	.00	2.30	56.23	38.98	.67	.17	.07	.70
	Average		.15	1.21	.23	3.02	61.11	33.76	.54	.22	.06	.50
2887	West Palm beach.	Pineapple land, 6"-30".	0.02	0.14	0.00	3.33	60.25	34.57	1.14	trace	trace	trace
2213	....do	Pineapple land, 12"-18".	.02	.12	.08	3.01	58.34	37.79	.23	0.05	0.13	0.20
2891	....do	Pineapple land, 6"-36".	.07	.07	.00	1.84	51.79	44.89	.94	.13	.08	.35
2214	....do	Pineapple land, subsoil.	.08	.30	.16	4.77	60.19	33.36	.30	.07	.31	.72
2889	....do	Pineapple land, 6"-36".	.18	.90	.04	2.45	56.92	38.28	.32	.12	.11	1.35
	Average		.07	.31	.06	3.08	57.50	37.78	.59	.07	.13	.52
2867	Rockledge	Spruce-pine scrub, 0"-6".	0.18	0.53	0.45	12.60	40.30	42.88	2.44	0.11	0.07	0.19
2865	....do	Spruce-pine scrub, 0"-6".	.11	1.59	.84	12.12	42.54	39.48	2.36	.21	.04	.50
	Average		.15	1.06	.65	12.36	41.42	41.18	2.40	.16	.06	.35
2866	Rockledge	Spruce-pine scrub, 6"-36".	0.25	0.45	0.66	9.07	32.58	52.13	3.26	0.23	0.18	0.51
2827	Ocala	Light hammock, 0"-9".	.35	1.16	trace	1.59	15.63	62.87	15.70	1.25	.48	.61
2871	Winterhaven	Light hammock, 0"-8".	.47	.59	trace	5.96	37.90	47.35	5.00	.73	.25	1.24
2830	Ocala, one-half mile south.	Light hammock, 0'-12".	.49	1.36	trace	3.07	21.44	53.54	13.30	2.68	1.33	2.39
2873	Winterhaven	Light hammock, 0'-9".	.66	2.39	trace	3.89	40.44	41.71	7.35	.84	.42	2.55
	Average		.49	1.48	trace	3.63	28.85	51.37	10.34	1.38	.62	1.70
2872	Winterhaven	Light hammock, 8"-36".	.62	.24	trace	6.46	42.00	43.49	3.96	.94	.23	1.21

Mechanical analyses of soils and subsoils—Continued.

No.	Locality.	Description.	Moisture in air-dry sample.	Organic matter.	Gravel (2–1 mm.).	Coarse sand (1–0.5 mm.).	Medium sand (0.5–0.25 mm.).	Fine sand (0.25–1 mm.).	Very fine sand (0.1–0.05 mm.).	Silt (0.05–0.01).	Fine silt (0.01–0.005 mm.).	Clay (0.005–0.0001 mm.).
			P. ct.	P. ct.	P. ct.	P. ct.	P. ct.	P. ct.	P. ct.	P. ct.	P. ct.	P. ct.
2829	Ocala	Light hammock, 24"–36".	0.30	0.65	trace	1.45	19.63	62.40	11.65	1.80	0.62	1.26
2828	...do	Light hammock, 9"–24".	.22	.75	trace	1.80	18.25	65.37	10.07	1.20	.55	1.39
2847	Silverspring	Light hammock, 12"–24".	.19	.40	.62	5.57	28.66	52.74	9.84	.38	.20	1.82
2831	Ocala, one-half mile south.	Light hammock, 12"–30".	.32	.92	.28	3.30	22.29	55.29	10.64	2.62	1.64	3.06
2874	Winterhaven	Light hammock, 9"–30".	.48	1.27	trace	3.74	38.30	43.47	7.67	.87	.28	3.68
		Average	.26	.71	.15	3.72	28.19	53.79	8.97	1.30	.59	2.07
2895	Quincy	Lafayette, 0"–12"	.33	1.63	.13	1.61	9.48	56.76	20.82	3.75	.81	4.37
2897	...do	Lafayette, 0"–12"	.84	4.35	1.01	5.35	18.33	40.86	14.49	4.31	.99	7.95
2899	...do	Lafayette, 0"–9"	.71	3.32	.45	2.10	19.25	47.37	15.28	4.99	.92	5.61
2901	...do	Lafayette, soil	.43	1.41	1.11	10.33	33.07	37.18	9.14	3.53	.49	2.65
		Average	.58	2.68	.68	4.85	20.03	45.53	14.93	4.15	.80	5.15
2895	Quincy	Lafayette, 12"–36"	.53	4.00	.18	1.45	9.38	46.30	14.16	4.70	.88	18.16
2900	...do	Lafayette, 9"–30"	1.31	5.89	.59	1.55	8.11	34.36	15.27	3.48	.77	29.15
2896	...do	Lafayette, subsoil	1.31	5.94	.51	1.24	6.06	33.41	13.58	2.79	1.74	34.15
2898	...do	Lafayette, 12"–12"	1.55	6.92	.88	3.52	11.68	26.54	10.54	2.51	.88	35.73
		Average	1.18	5.69	.54	1.94	8.81	35.15	13.39	3.37	1.07	29.30
2857	Rockledge	Heavy (gray) hammock, 0"–18".	.26	.92	.18	4.80	31.31	58.80	2.07	.23	.09	.85
2319	Fort Meade	Heavy (gray) hammock, 0"–33".	1.06	2.50	.80	3.81	13.77	50.10	24.41	.90	.55	.99
2859	Rockledge	Heavy (gray) hammock, 0"–18".	.13	.74	.16	3.50	33.00	61.19	.98	.18	.83	1.03
2820	Fort Meade	Heavy (gray) hammock, 0"–20".	1.39	2.88	.25	1.36	7.76	41.75	41.22	1.22	.70	1.58
2817	...do	Heavy (gray) hammock, 0"–20".	.94	2.13	.41	2.97	12.92	48.99	26.69	.74	.30	3.93
		Average	.76	1.84	.36	3.29	19.75	52.17	19.08	.66	.50	1.68
2860	Rockledge	Heavy (gray) hammock, 18"–30".	.27	.66	.19	3.99	28.76	63.78	1.42	.14	.14	.13
2858	...do	Heavy (gray) hammock, 18"–36".	.16	.55	.11	5.49	35.75	54.75	1.20	.01	.06	.14
2821	Fort Meade	Heavy (gray) hammock, 20"–36".	1.03	2.16	.36	1.40	8.30	48.87	35.36	1.00	.52	1.17
2818	...do	Heavy (gray) hammock, 20"–36".	1.06	3.06	.40	4.29	19.15	46.70	20.19	.78	.47	3.44
		Average	.63	1.61	.27	3.79	22.99	53.53	14.54	.48	.30	1.22
1621	Altoona	Etonia scrub, 0"–4"	.12	1.13	.56	3.43	35.90	51.00	6.27	1.01	.28	.54
2915	...do	Etonia scrub, 0"–3"	.34	1.78	.16	4.54	33.21	53.64	4.46	.41	.18	.64
2917	Orange City Junction	Etonia scrub, 0"–6"	.21	1.00	.00	.33	5.58	75.33	16.66	.40	.18	.75
2913	Altoona	Etonia scrub, 0"–4'	.19	1.04	.18	5.06	35.03	54.44	3.02	.37	.15	1.53
		Average	.22	1.24	.23	3.34	27.43	58.60	7.60	.55	.20	.87
1622	Altoona	Etonia scrub, 6"–18".	.68	1.13	.34	3.92	40.39	44.97	6.96	.79	.33	1.16
2916	...do	Etonia scrub, 3"–30".	.05	1.78	.27	4.87	36.31	51.69	2.14	1.34	.10	1.45
2918	Orange City Junction	Etonia scrub, 6"–36".	.17	1.00	.00	.23	5.70	79.84	11.46	.52	.27	1.73
2914	Altoona	Etonia scrub, 4"–36".	.17	1.04	.34	4.94	36.15	53.16	2.82	.32	.18	1.90
		Average	.28	1.24	.24	3.49	29.64	57.47	5.85	.74	.22	1.56
2861	Rockledge	Red coquina hammock, 0"–6".	.93	3.64	.06	10.85	37.31	38.34	5.50	.67	.19	1.03
2863	...do	Red coquina hammock, 0"–4".	1.54	6.85	.68	10.44	28.05	39.38	9.93	.95	.39	1.62
		Average	1.24	5.25	.67	10.65	32.67	38.86	7.72	.81	.29	1.33

30

Mechanical analyses of soils and subsoils—Continued.

No.	Locality.	Description.	Moisture in air-dry sample.	Organic matter.	Gravel (2-1 mm.).	Coarse sand (1-0.5 mm.).	Medium sand (0.5-0.25 mm.).	Fine sand (0.25-1 mm.).	Very fine sand (0.1-0.05 mm.).	Silt (0.05-0.01 mm.).
			P. ct.	P. ct.	P. ct.	P. ct.	P. ct.	P. ct.	P. ct.	P. ct.
2862	Rockledge	Red coquina hammock, 6″-36″.	0.52	0.67	0.78	12.56	36.93	41.46	4.56	0.45
2864	.....do	Red coquina hammock, 4″-18″.	.55	2.02	.49	9.35	27.59	46.58	8.67	1.15
		Average	.53	1.35	.64	15.96	32.26	44.02	6.62	.80
2822	Fort Meade..	Mulatto hammock 0″-12″.	.62	1.53	.78	2.85	14.35	53.51	23.50	.65
2823	Fort Meade...	Mulatto hammock subsoil.	.47	1.43	.70	2.50	14.30	53.00	24.46	.62
2869	Grand Island.	High pine land, 0″-8″.	.12	1.43	7.60	18.32	27.88	38.45	3.35	.86
1619	Altoona	High pine land, 0″-6″.	.23	1.27	1.98	5.18	12.93	27.48	45.87	2.78
2875	Winterhaven.	High pine land, 0″-8″.	.26	1.31	.01	2.88	35.01	51.28	7.70	.75
1623	Eustis........	High pine land, 0″-6″.	.54	1.75	2.31	11.52	44.76	30.90	4.40	1.14
2911	Altoona	High pine land, 0″-4″.	.25	1.25	.47	7.49	38.09	49.42	2.29	.31
2879	Winterhaven.	High pine land,[2] 0″-8″.	.13	.80	.05	7.66	44.40	40.52	4.66	.51
2906	Altoona	High pine land, 0″-8″.	.47	1.65	1.39	3.51	8.71	55.17	26.21	.93
2908	.....do	High pine land, 0″-8″.	.39	2.00	2.61	4.64	13.69	60.28	15.33	.60
2826	Fort Meade...	High pine land,[2] 0″-18″.	.47	1.60	.10	.65	4.58	47.88	40.90	.58
2824	Fort Meade. one-half mile south.	High pine land,[1] 0″-20″.	1.54	3.02	.52	2.94	16.00	47.95	24.73	.86
2852	Bartow	High pine land, 0″-9″.	.81	3.37	.35	2.21	20.83	46.70	21.89	1.24
2850	.....do	High pine land, 0″-9″.	.55	2.44	.17	2.31	19.74	45.32	25.71	.97
		Average	.48	1.82	1.46	5.78	23.89	45.11	18.42	.96
2912	Altoona	High pine land, 4″-30″.	.13	.53	.63	7.30	34.92	51.11	3.47	.44
2870	Grand Island.	High pine land, 8″-36″.	.14	.65	7.40	15.87	24.63	44.09	3.87	1.12
1624	Eustis........	High pine land, 6″-18″.	.25	.66	2.74	11.70	42.05	35.29	4.50	.88
2909	Altoona	High pine land, 8″-36″.	.16	.68	2.69	5.27	13.01	61.92	14.64	.75
2876	Winterhaven	High pine land, 8″-36″.	.12	.32	.03	3.59	37.41	48.77	7.88	.66
2907	Altoona	High pine land, 8″-36″.	.29	.67	1.89	3.34	6.86	53.30	29.71	1.20
1620	.....do	High pine land, 6″-18″.	.15	.87	1.61	4.52	12.28	27.58	48.12	2.16
2880	Winterhaven.	High pine land,[2] 8″-30″.	.16	.36	.16	9.70	47.41	37.72	2.76	.48
2920	Fort Meade...	High pine land,[2] 18″-36″.	.30	.82	.11	.71	6.19	64.37	24.59	.73
2825	Fort Meade. one-half mile south.	High pine land,[1] 20″-30″.	.48	2.22	.52	3.14	17.23	49.29	23.14	.62
2853	Bartow	High pine land, 9″-30″.	.54	1.24	.24	1.61	17.91	49.22	24.98	.78
2851	.....do	High pine land, 9″-30″.	.36	1.09	.10	1.83	19.57	48.41	23.66	.65
		Average	.28	.84	1.51	5.72	23.29	47.51	17.61	.87
2837	Ocala	Mixed lands, 0″-12″.	.39	1.63	.09	4.07	32.31	44.72	11.10	2.55
2845	.....do	Mixed lands, soil.....	.31	1.34	.10	1.95	24.46	60.25	9.59	.42

[1] First quality high pine land.　　　　[2] Third quality high pine land.

Mechanical analyses of soils and subsoils—Continued.

No.	Locality.	Description.	Moisture in air-dry sample.	Organic matter.	Gravel (2-1 mm.).	Coarse sand (1-0.5 mm.).	Medium sand (0.5-0.25 mm.).	Fine sand (0.25-1 mm.).	Very fine sand (0.1-0.05 mm.).	Silt (0.05-0.01 mm.).	Fine silt (0.01-0.005 mm.).	Clay (0.005-0.0001 mm.).
			P. ct.	P. ct.	P. ct.	P. ct.	P. ct.	P. ct.	P. ct.	P. ct.	P. ct.	P. ct.
2839	Ocala, 2 miles south.	Mixed lands, 0″–12″..	0.78	1.56	trace	2.12	16.88	57.57	11.30	2.26	1.27	5.19
2842	Ocala.........	Mixed lands, 0″–9″..	1.11	3.46	trace	3.50	32.95	34.15	10.64	2.96	.95	9.63
	Average.		.65	2.00	.05	2.91	26.65	49.17	10.66	2.05	.74	4.75
2838	Ocala.........	Mixed lands, 12″–36″.	.06	.49	trace	3.15	24.94	51.10	13.47	2.33	1.10	2.29
2841	Ocala, 2 miles south.	Mixed lands, 24″–36″.	.41	1.10	trace	1.90	13.83	63.70	12.85	2.06	.94	2.48
2846	Ocala.........	Mixed lands, subsoil.	.24	.72	.32	2.42	27.55	57.44	6.84	.50	.24	3.00
2840	Ocala, 2 miles south.	Mixed lands, 12″–24″.	.19	.72	trace	1.95	13.15	62.53	12.35	1.81	.87	5.85
2843	Ocala.........	Mixed lands, 9″–24...	1.41	3.20	trace	3.67	30.80	33.00	9.45	2.24	.87	14.66
	Average.		.46	1.25	.06	2.62	22.05	53.55	10.99	1.79	.80	5.66
1625	Altoona.......	Rich heavy hammock, 0″–6″.	.16	1.38	.96	.22	12.52	46.50	29.69	2.07	.50	.92
2884	Orange Bend.	Rich heavy hammock, 0″–8″.	.44	1.77	.45	4.92	35.77	42.85	6.49	2.33	.54	4.58
2834	Ocala.........	Rich heavy hammock, 0″–12″.	1.61	4.94	.27	2.16	17.01	40.94	20.26	5.61	2.23	5.55
2832	Ocala, 2½ miles south.	Rich heavy hammock, 0″–12″.	1.39	2.61	1.58	2.62	13.08	46.32	19.83	3.38	1.50	6.86
	Average.		.90	2.68	.82	2.48	19.60	44.15	19.07	3.35	1.19	4.48

www.ingramcontent.com/pod-product-compliance
Lightning Source LLC
Chambersburg PA
CBHW021448090426
42739CB00009B/1684